TABLE OF CONTENTS
PART 1

SCAN ME

video performance

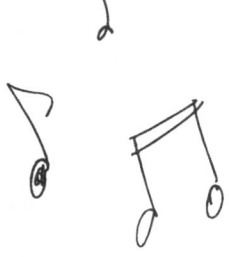

TABLE OF CONTENTS
PART 2

SCAN ME

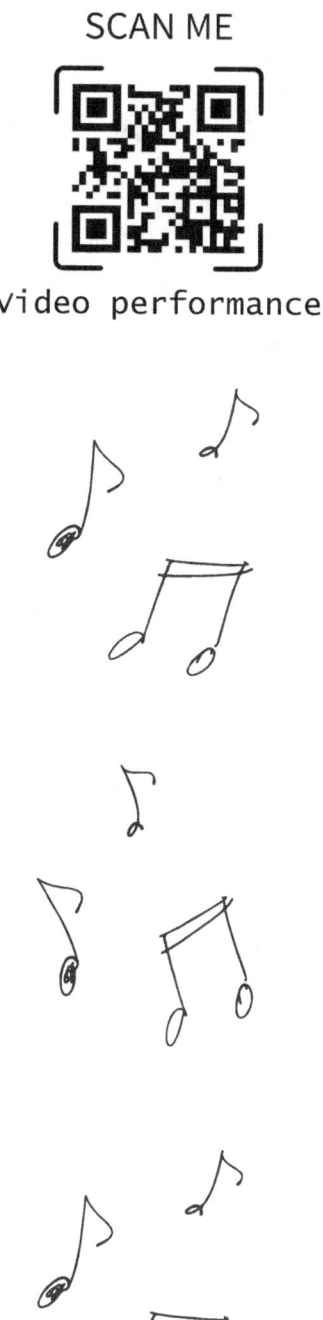

video performance

HELENA D

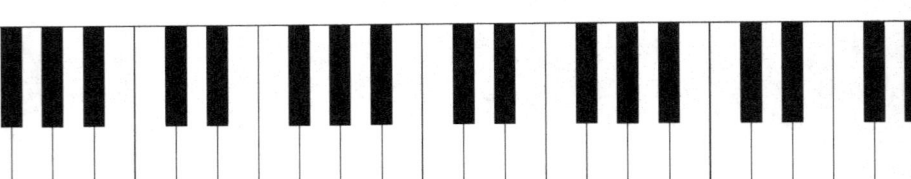

MUSICIAN
COMPOSER
PIANO TEACHER

This book is a joyful journey into the world of piano for children. Inside you will find 20 original piano pieces that vary in style, character, and technical focus. Each composition is thoughtfully crafted to help young pianists gradually explore different aspects of piano technique: hand coordination, finger agility, dynamics, articulation, phrasing, and expressive playing.

The collection is more than just a set of exercises — it is an invitation to imagination. Every piece is paired with a unique coloring page, carefully designed to reflect the spirit of the music.

As children play and then color the picture, they connect sound and image, strengthening their emotional bond with the music. This creative combination encourages them not only to practice but also to dream, visualize, and tell their own stories through both art and sound.

Teachers will find this collection a valuable tool, as it allows them to introduce new skills in a fun and memorable way. Students will love the diversity of pieces — some are playful and energetic, others lyrical and dreamy, and some even humorous or mysterious. With every page, children experience music not only as notes on paper, but as a living, colorful adventure.

Holiday Gift

Helena D

Allegretto

Butterfly Dance

Helena D

Daddy

Helena D

Allegretto

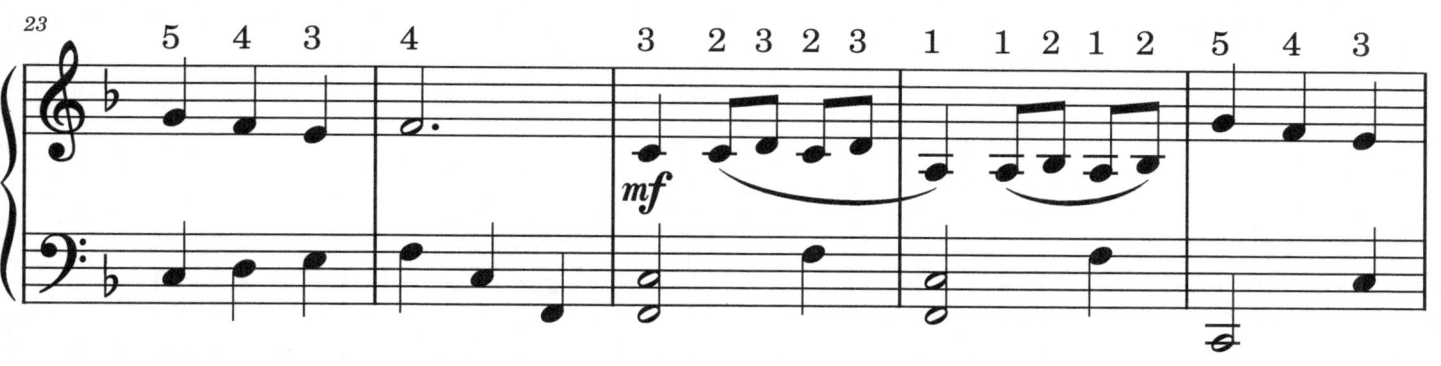

Mommy

Helena D

9

Gift For Grandma

Helena D

Moderato

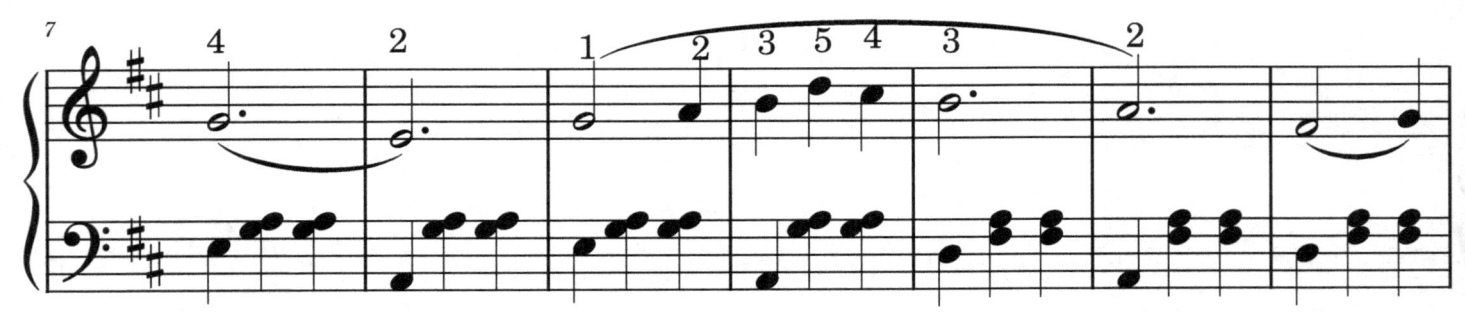

First Snow

Helena D

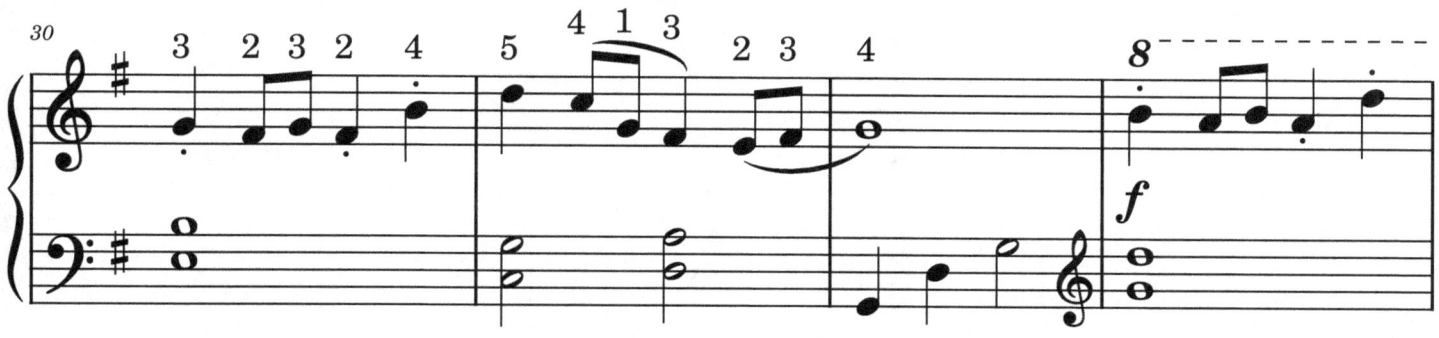

Harlequin

Helena D

Allegretto

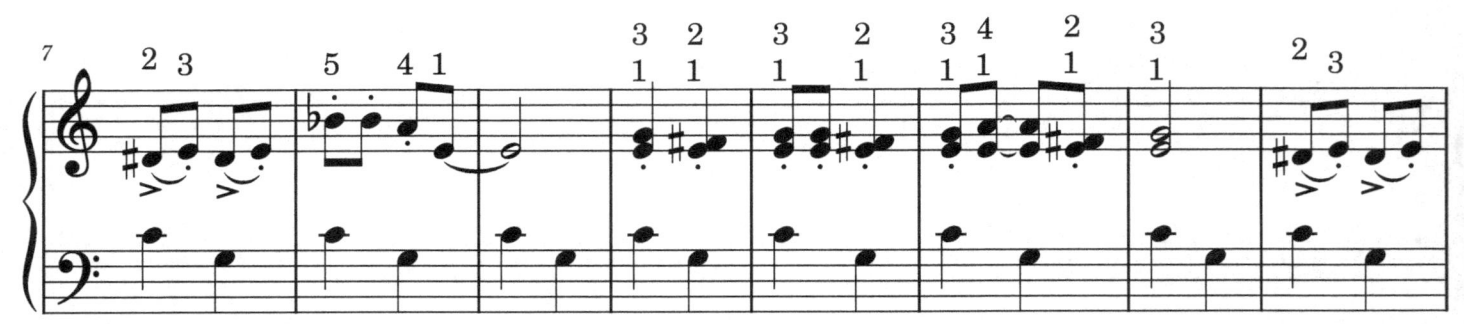

Rainbow Chase

Helena D

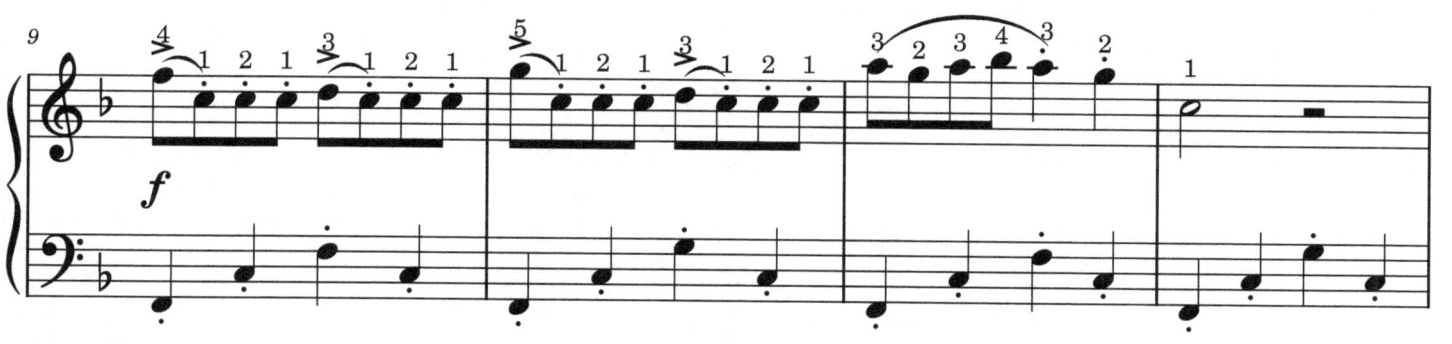

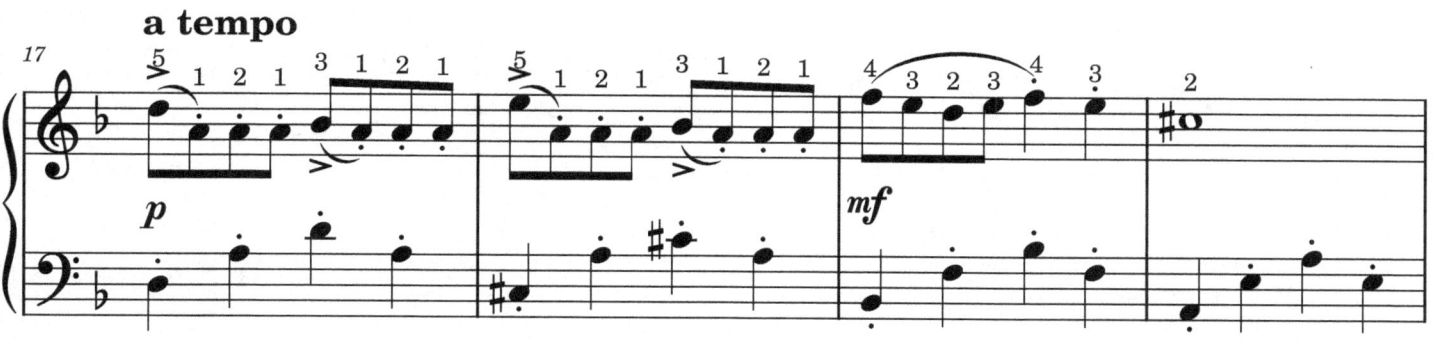

Mysterious Music Box

Helena D

Adagio

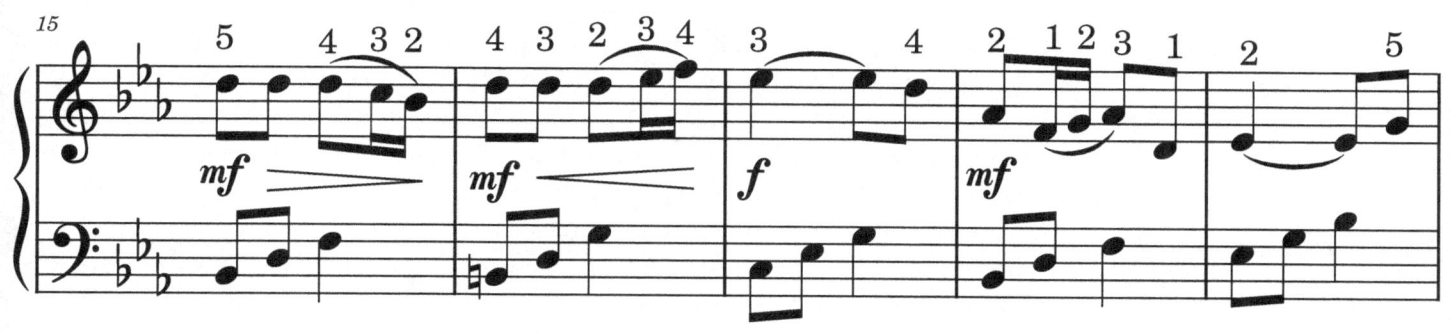

rit. _ _ _ _ _ _ _   a tempo

Little Fantasy

Helena D

Allegretto

Travel

Helena D

Puppy

Helena D

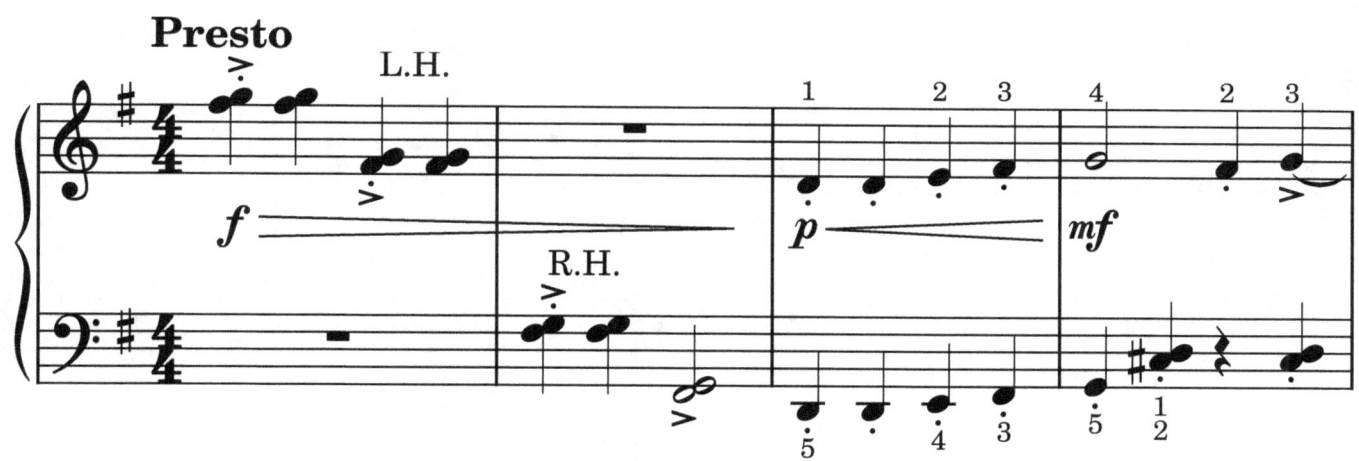

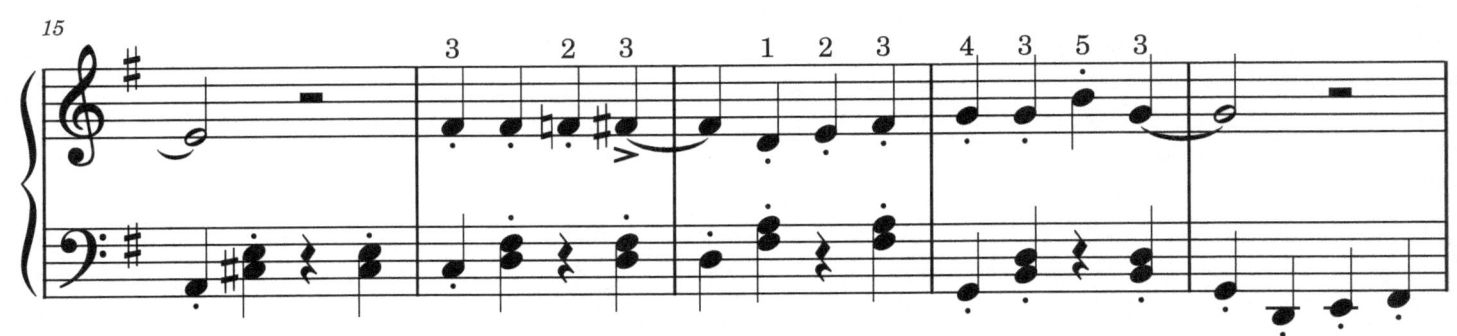

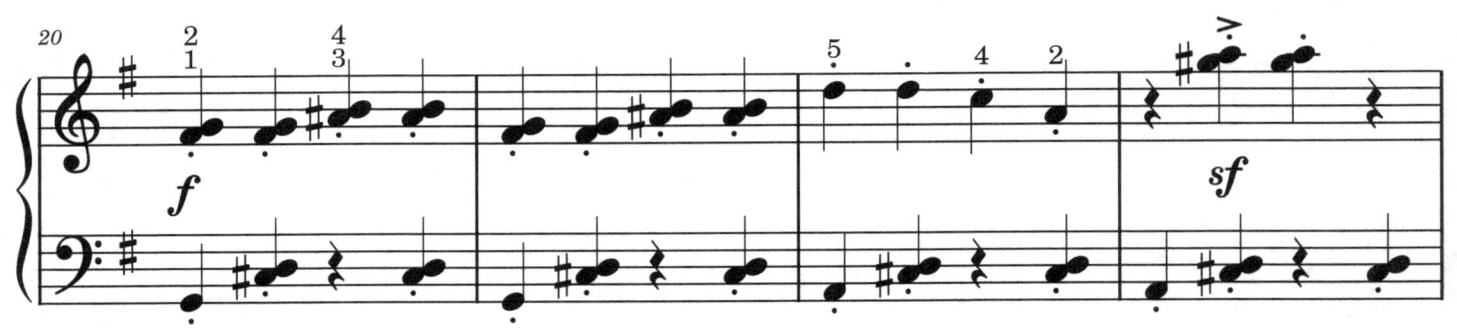

Dance with a Fan

Helena D

Allegro

The Pirate

Helena D

The Princess

Helena D

Vivace

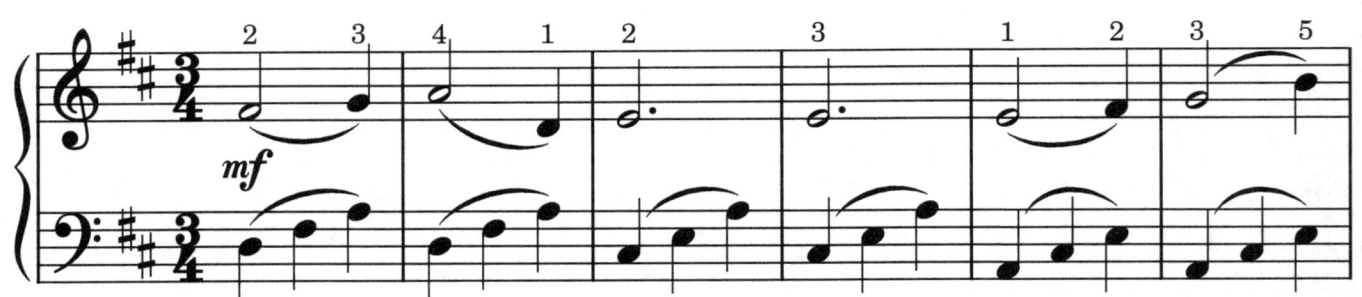

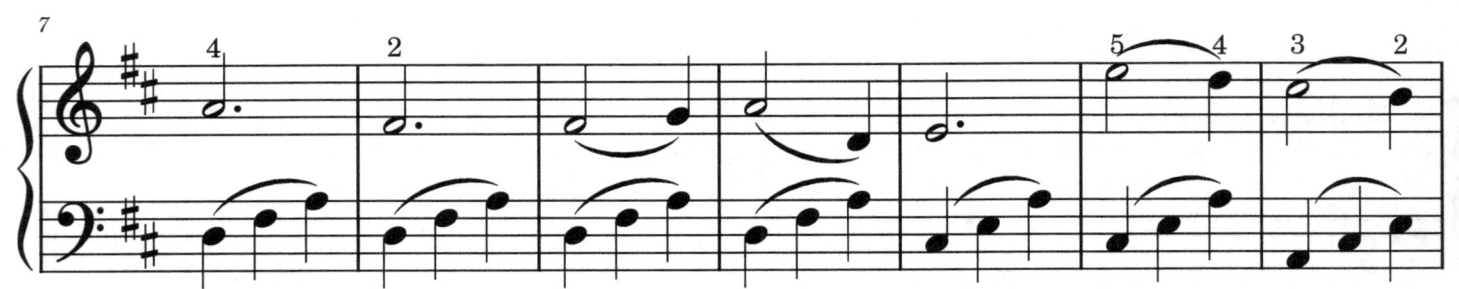

We Went On Vacation

Helena D

Allegro

Waltz

Helena D

Vivace

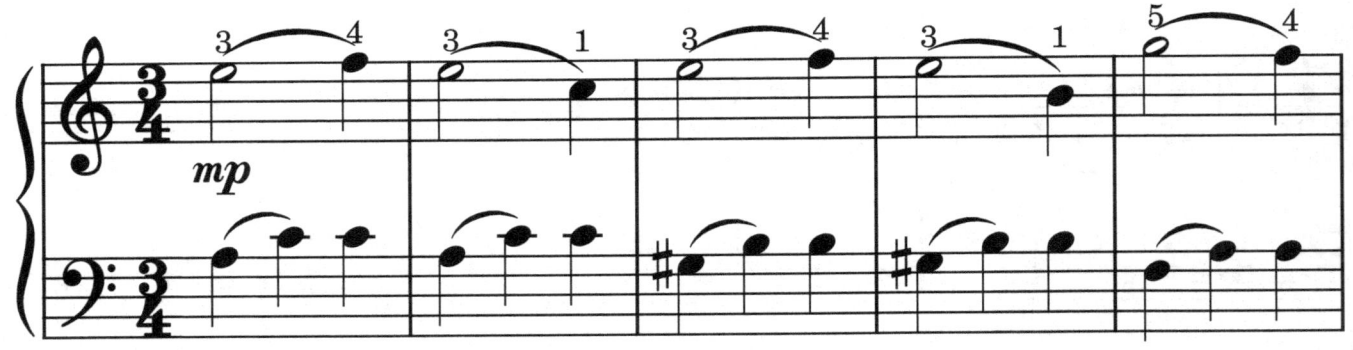

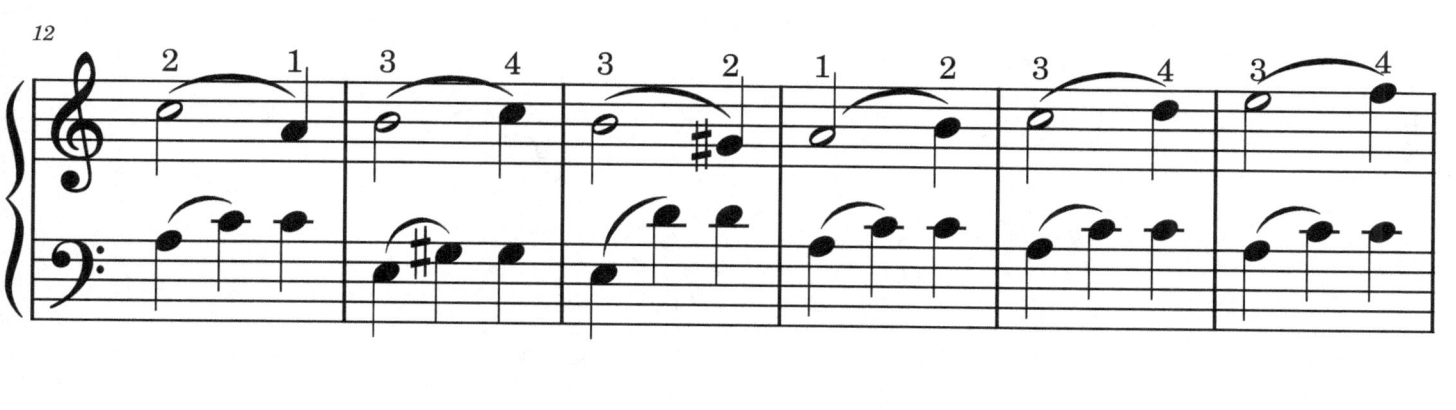

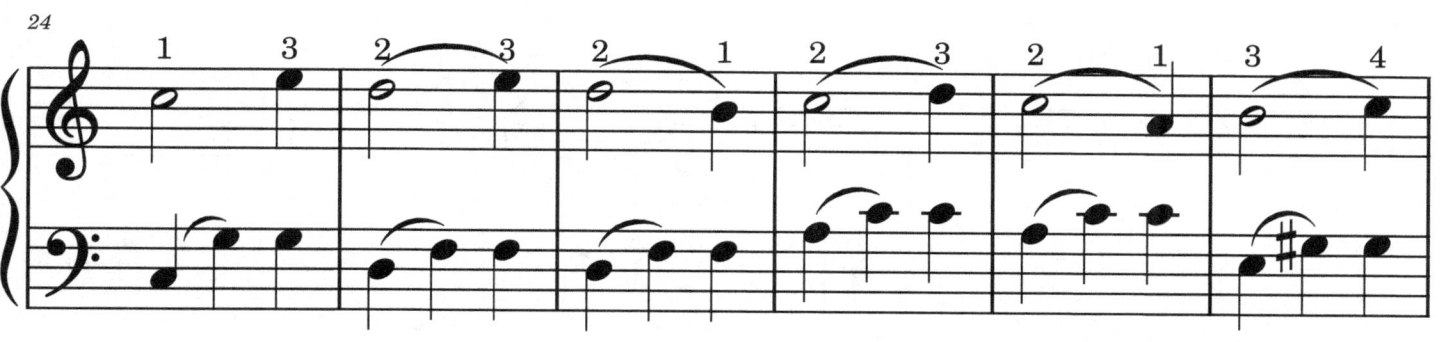

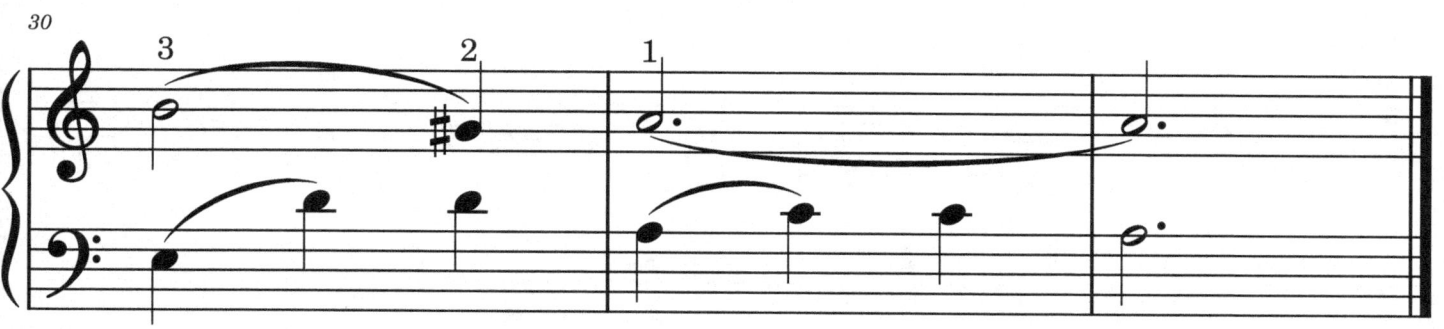

Jumping in Puddles

Helena D

Run and Catch

Helena D

Allegretto

43

On the Farm

Helena D

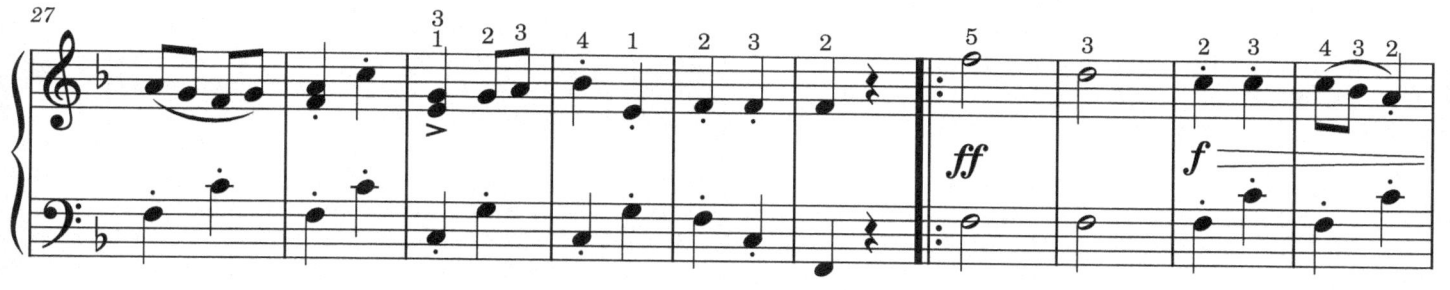

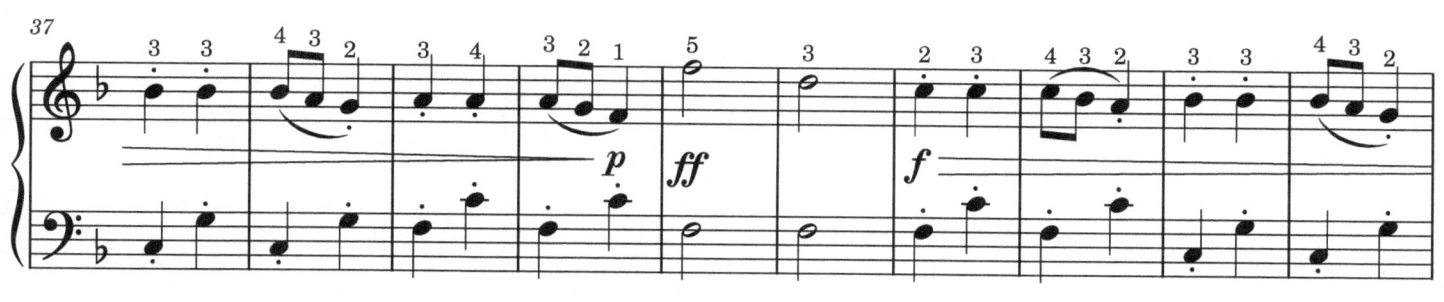

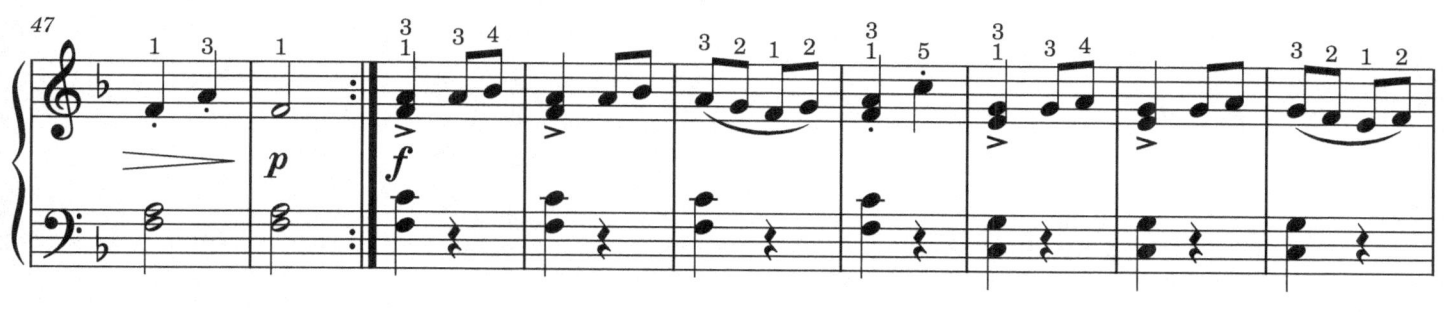

Workbook Overview & Purpose

This workbook was created to be used in companion with the comprehensive, educational book, *Question Everything: Advice for Students and Graduates!*

Both books are **dedicated to the student who lives within each of us.** Let us remain inquisitive by questioning all things, thoughts, traditions, ideas, habits, patterns, systems, and rules! As we graduate to new levels of life, we must continue to challenge any self-imposed, familial, proximal, or societal limitations.

Please understand that **SCHOOL AND EDUCATION ARE NOT THE SAME THING!** With the proper advice, mindset, and techniques, anyone can become educated; with or without school. Both books include the applicable, helpful, practical, real, and transparent advice that the author would tell his younger self.

THIS BOOK BELONGS TO:

_ _

Ordering Information:
Quantity sales. Special discounts are available on quantity purchases by corporations, associations, and others. For details, contact the email address above.

Printed in the United States of America
Published by CM Book Publishing

First printing, 2025

ISBN: 979-8-9929468-8-8